Influential Pain

Rachel Whittenburg

Butterfly Wings Publishing

Influential Pain
All Rights Reserved.
Copyright © 2023 Rachel Whittenburg
v1.0

The opinions expressed in this manuscript are solely the opinions of the author and do not represent the opinions or thoughts of the publisher. The author has represented and warranted full ownership and/or legal right to publish all the materials in this book.

This book may not be reproduced, transmitted, or stored in whole or in part by any means, including graphic, electronic, or mechanical without the express written consent of the publisher except in the case of brief quotations embodied in critical articles and reviews.

Butterfly Wings Publishing

ISBN: 978-0-578-27587-1

Cover Photo © 2023 Rachel Whittenburg. All rights reserved - used with permission.

PRINTED IN THE UNITED STATES OF AMERICA

Dedicated in memory of my mother.
Patricia Ann Treadway
March 30,1938 November 4, 1980

TABLE OF CONTENTS

CHAPTER ONE 1
CHAPTER TWO.. 4
CHAPTER THREE 8
CHAPTER FOUR 13
CHAPTER FIVE 19
CHAPTER SIX 23
CHAPTER SEVEN 26
CHAPTER EIGHT.. 30
CHAPTER NINE.. 33
CHAPTER TEN.. 35
CHAPTER ELEVEN... 40
CHAPTER TWELVE 42
CHAPTER FOURTEEN 44
CHAPTER FIFTEEN 48
CHAPTER SIXTEEN... 51
QUOTES 55

CHAPTER ONE

BEFORE I START sharing my story I'm going to introduce you to my family by sharing with you who they are as persons. I'll start off with my father and so on. I'll need to tell you a few things about my family's dynamics before I start sharing my life story with you. My name is Rebekah, I'm 54 years old and have four children biologically and a son who became part of our family in 2002 for a total of five. I have two daughters and three sons.

I grew up in a family with very different dynamics. There were five of us in all. Now I will tell you a story of how one traumatic experience changed my life and the life of my family.

I can remember back to the age of three or four. My father worked on a minnow farm outside the small town of Hazen, Arkansas. He was provided with a farm house to live in and there was also a barn with a small herd of cattle.

He was a man of tall stature, around six foot or so. He weighed around two hundred pounds with broad shoulders. He had blue eyes and his hair was thinning on top. He was of German descent and had pale skin. One thing I can remember very well--he had beautiful teeth. He was well groomed and shaven. He always wore khaki pants and shirt with boots. He was honest above all, which was very hard for me to wrap my head around as I got older. He worked and provided for our family above the average in our region. Though he only had a fifth grade education he could read or write anything. My Uncle Alfred always said he had all the marbles out of the bunch.

INFLUENTIAL PAIN

Like any child, a considerable amount of my childhood was about my father--his beliefs, his nature, and his character. He did not believe in doctors or celebrating Christmas. He was raised old fashioned and believed in directing you only once and he never said 'I love you.' I know my older sister was his favorite because he always did more for her than the rest of the children. My oldest brother and youngest brother would suffer from the physical abuse the most. My mother always made sure my older brother would receive better because of it.

My father was raised in an environment more hostile than most know. He was the oldest of seven children. My grandparents were poor and lived off the White river. The family would catch and barrel net fish for a living, our main source of income. I can only tell what I know by hearsay and the very few times I was around them. They were very strict or, as I would say, just mean. I do know that when any of the children did wrong my grandfather would hit them in the head with a boat paddle. They were not family-oriented with any of their children or grandchildren. Out of seven children, four would become alcoholics. It's my understanding that my grandmother went to church but did not hold to, "practicing what you preach." It only made my father meaner and very cold-hearted.

He was also the oldest and I know he was raised in a verbal and physically abusive atmosphere. I was told that my grandfather would hit the boys in the head with a boat paddle when something wasn't done right. There were six boys and one girl--she was the baby of the bunch. I remember my grandparents—I was older when they passed. It's a funny thing. They were not the usual grandparents that most chidren have. The relationship between them and their children was really strange. I never understood it and never will.

Let me tell you a little bit about my mother and what she was like. She was a short, petite woman with beautiful dark coal black hair, dark brown eyes and brown olive skin. There was no doubt there was Cherokee indian in her blood. I do know she grabbed attention from many men. That can be a blessing when you're a beautiful woman or it can be your worst curse.

CHAPTER ONE

She was very intelligent and started one project and mastered it before she moved on to the next. She earned her beautician license to cut hair. She also taught at a beauty school at Stuttgart. Then she decided to take classes for decorating cakes. Cake-baking was her focus for about six months. I can remember a wedding cake she made with a water fountain on top of the bottom layer. It was amazing to me.

She came from a family of money and workers who truly earned their money. My grandfather, El Tacker, had a restaurant in the 1950s called Jeff's Lunch Cart. It was located on highway 70 between DeValls Bluff and Hazen. It was a diner cart and was very popular. Highway 70 was the main route to Memphis, Tennessee before Interstate 40 was developed.

I learned that my maternal grandmother, Violet, was an alcoholic. There were four girls and two boys, and my mother was second oldest. They were considered a family of wealth in that time and era. Nice home, vehicles and nice clothing. The family seemed to come from money on my grandfather's side. But like I said, his brothers and himself earned their money and were self-made men. My grandfather, El, would pass away before I was born and my grandmother, Violet, a couple years after my birth. I do not remember her at all.

There are pictures, history pieces, newspaper articles and memorabilia at Prairie County Museums and Prairie County Courthouses including Jeff's Lunch Cart, from the 1950s. It was a pleasant surprise for me to learn about my grandparents. My mother had never told us anything.....EVER!

CHAPTER TWO

THE FIRST CHILD my parents birthed would be a girl, Maureen. She was twelve years older than me, so quite the age difference. She's around 5'7" or so in height. Maureen inherited more the German gene from our side of the family. She has the pale skin and is bigger boned in stature. She married at sixteen years of age and moved out when I was around four years old. She is one of stubborn nature and has a really hard time claiming responsibility when she is to blame. My sister doesn't like to be at fault. I think in her mind it makes her feel like she's not a good person, and she will argue the point and it's absolutely a waste of time. She's not going to hear it.

She married at sixteen years of age to a man who would be eleven years older. Lynn was a mechanic and worked for his uncle in the small town of Hazen. Lynn was liked by everyone in town. He was a good-natured guy and kind to all.

She would have her first child, a daughter, at the age of seventeen and a son at the age of twenty-one. Our family loved Lynn and he was good to us kids. Their marriage would dissolve in divorce after twenty years. The family always remained in contact with Lynn and he always remained good to us up until his death in October of 2008.

My brother, Albert, was eleven years older. He was about 5'7, I'm guessing, with blonde hair, blue eyes, and olive skin. His frame was thin and lanky which was often inherited from our father's side. He was a little more on the wilder side, full of adventure, and carried no fear of conseqences for his actions. He would often move out of state and lived in California. He was not on good terms with the law in Arkansas and was arrested for selling marijuana. He would be bi-polar and use drugs that would speed him up to keep him feeling 'normal' mentally. It would become a problem for many years and alcohol was often used to cope.

Albert would finally get married and have three lovely children. Their marriage came with plenty of ups and downs due to the undiagnosed bi-polar disorder and doctors did not have much medical knowledge in that time to treat the disorder. The marriage would end in divorce and he remarried another later. The next fourteen years would be different due to being diagnosed and getting on proper medication. He became the person we all knew he could be. He would still trip up occasionally but would get back up again. Ten of those years he spent fighting health issues. A large portion of time was spent in hospitals and doctors' offices.

At the age of fifty, I would lose Albert to a cerebral stroke. It was very painful and I grieved for a long time. We had grown very close as I grew older. His funeral would be considered large with over two hundred guests. His compassion and caring for people during those final years proved to be honorable in some eyes.

Abel is my second oldest brother. He was fourteen months older so it made us close growing up. He was about 5'8, small frame, thin and lanky as well. He had dark brown hair, brown eyes and that olive skin. Abel was born with a kidney disease in which his kidneys were turned backwards. He was about five years old when my parents found out he was sick. Because of being sick, he was smaller than most children our age.

Abel was rustic, as they would say. He loved to fish and hunt. He was good at doing both. He was quiet and one rarely heard him complain. He was very calm and protective of his family. I could never really get him to talk much. He wasn't one who got mad easily and was compassionate when it came to helping someone out. I think he accepted his illness and didn't take much for granted. He was just a good old-fashioned country boy.

INFLUENTIAL PAIN

Abel would pass in 2008, at the age of forty-two. He had been put back on dialysis and grew tired of it all. Abel and I had a long talk about it before he decided to quit dialysis. He grew tired of being sick and in and out of hospitals all his life. I could understand completely because he had no life. What kind life is it if you're spending most of your time enduring surgeries and hospital stays? It's the most COURAGE I've seen anyone display, knowing death was absolute and being absolutely fearless of it.

I would be the fourth child for my parents. My entering the world was different than most. My father would be taking my mother to Brinkley Hospital, when he would have to pull over in the Baptist Church parking lot in Fredonia, also known as Biscoe, Arkansas.

It was April of 1967, cold and with snow on the ground. This is what we also call a blackberry winter in Arkansas and most southern states. It was around 1:00 a.m. in the morning and my father would deliver me in the front seat of the truck. The story was told that he had to fight off a pack of wild dogs during this whole time. He would cut the umbilical cord with pocket knife and tie it with a red handkerchief he carried in his pocket.

After my delivery, my father would take my mother to Brinkley Hospital about 20 minutes away. The doctor told my father everything looked good and he'd done a good job delivering me. A few weeks later my mother would develop gangrene from the afterbirth not being cleaned out of the womb properly.

I am around five feet and a half inch tall with olive skin, long dark brown hair and dark brown eyes. I was born with a birthmark on my right cheek which was about the size of a nickel. I was very petite in size and that was normal from my mother's side of the family. Being around two brothers growing up, I was a tomboy. We fished, hunted and trapped during the winter to make money. Abel and I trapped every year. My father always believed someone should bring something to the table if they expected to eat from the table.

Paul was youngest of us all, the baby of the bunch. He's fourteen months younger than I. The average height of all three boys was 5'7

CHAPTER TWO

or 5'8. Paul had blonde hair, blue eyes, a thin frame and lanky build. He would be the best looking of the boys, rather handsome and had a persuasive tongue. He could talk you out of the shirt on your back and make you believe it was fair.

Paul was spoiled, ornery and very much into being rebellious. He did whatever he wanted and when he wanted. In other words, he was mean as a snake. He wouldn't listen to reason from anyone and usually stayed in trouble probably because he intended to do it his way or no way. Abel and I often covered for him because the consequences would be harsher than he deserved. There were countless times we both did this over the years of growing and even into adult life.

Paul now struggles with many mental issues, dishonesty and thievery. He has been diagnosed with bi-polar, schizophrenia, psychosis with homicidal tendencies. Although he is on medication, the problem is he will not take it properly and some things you just can't change or help. You finally learn as an adult to leave it alone.

Paul has lived a life the past twenty years in and out of jail, always into some kind of trouble. He's lived the homeless life in different small towns and has lived the way we never wanted to see one of our family members live. I hope and pray he finds his way. Living wrong and doing wrong never leads to a good life. It's his life and his choices and I learned to accept that.

CHAPTER THREE

MY DAD WORKED for a man named Martin Fry on a minnow farm and he also had a small herd of cattle. We lived in a farmhouse that went with the job. It was something that all farmers provided for their employees. In those days having a home included with your job was a big deal and helped families to make ends meet at the end of each month.

I can remember while living there, Abel, Paul and myself playing outside often. One of our favorite things to play was crop-dusting. We put dirt in our underwear and spread our arms out like airplanes, running as fast as we could and watching the dust fly from behind us. It was lots of fun. When I grew up children mostly played outside and knew how to entertain themselves. Times have changed since then.

Unexpectedly, Abel, Paul and myself would be a second family for my parents. The house we lived in had two bedrooms, but they were big. I shared a room with both of my brothers. Ironically we are all fourteen months apart in age. It was very common back then for siblings to share rooms. I never really understood why Abel had to sleep in a baby bed. I only knew he wet the bed every night and that my father would spank him every morning because of it. I look back now and realize it was just short of a beating. This was repetitious until Abel was about five years old. I guess my mom had reached a breaking point and took Abel to a small town doctor in Hazen. This doctor saved my brother's life. The doctor told

CHAPTER THREE

my mother to take Abel to Stuttgart Hospital immediately. I didn't understand a lot about why my mother was going through this with my father, but I definitely understand it now.

At Stuttgart Hospital mom sat and waited for a few hours while various tests were given to Abel. The doctor then told my mother that Abel needed to go to UAMS in Little Rock. Abel was admitted immediately into the hospital. Abel was very sick. As I mentioned, he was born with a birth defect where his kidneys were turned backwards. (Ectopic kidneys are more likely to have vesicoureteral reflux. VUR is a condition in which urine flows backward from the bladder to one or both ureters and sometimes the kidneys).

However, the stay would be a long one. I don't know how many surgeries Abel had at the time. I only know his stay in the hospital would be over a year. I remember we'd go see him on the weekends. He was in a room by himself with glass windows and we were not allowed to go in. I could not imagine how hard this was on him at such a young age. It would be several months later before he was able to come out of the room for a few minutes to visit. The risk of infection was a real concern to Dr. Redmond.

I do know that by the time he was twenty-one years old, Abel had been through twenty-six surgeries and one later—thus totaling twenty-seven all together During Abel's hospital stay, my father, James was offered a better job. He would manage a minnow farm for Mr. Leland Mathers. Mr. Mathers was quadriplegic due to an airplane crash when he was a few years younger. This job would offer a new home on five acres and a percentage of sales every year from what the farm would yield plus bonuses.

The minnow farm had an office and just a few minnow vats that were already built. My father would finish the minnow vats and start on creating minnow ponds. There were two ponds by the shop and several others a few miles away from the shop. My father would build two more buildings for making mats for minnows to lay eggs on. My father turned that farm into a money-making business.

Abel remained in the hospital while we moved and got settled in

INFLUENTIAL PAIN

before he would be able to come home from the hospital. My father bought a building and made it into a beauty shop for my mother. We lived about twenty miles from the town of Des Arc. That was the start of a new life for me, my brother, Paul, and my parents. It would seem that all those years of hard work my parents went through had finally paid off with a better future for the whole family.

A year and a few months later, Abel finally got out of the hospital and got to come home. He would have colostomy bags on each side that the urine would drain into. The colostomy bags would have to be changed out several times throughout the day. My father would change out almost every one like clockwork. I guess the guilt made him feel responsible. Abel would start school and we'd be in the same grade. I started kindergarten at Hazen Elementary School but it wouldn't be long after we moved that I would start at Des Arc Elementary School.

I felt really sad for Abel and tried to help him catch up on the school education he'd missed. Abel had a very difficult time catching up.

As a child you don't really see things the same way you do as an adult. I guess I really didn't know how sick Abel really was. I do know there were more surgeries and many more hospital stays through the school years.

A few years later my mom would decide to buy a local cafe in town. She sold her beauty shop and then began a minnow route around the same time she would purchase the cafe. I can remember in the afternoons after getting off of the school bus, Abel and I would have to go to the minnow shop and work for dad there. On the weekends my mother had me working at the cafe. Neither Abel nor I got paid for working. Our pay was a roof over our head and food on the table—old fashioned beliefs.

This was the normal routine for me up until that one morning which would change everything. One early morning, out of the blue I woke up to my mother screaming. It also awakened Abel. We went into the kitchen and our father was hitting our mother. It was scary

CHAPTER THREE

and just didn't seem real. This was my father, who always made it clear to all of us children, that arguing or disagreements between him and Mom were carried on behind closed doors. Believe it when I tell you, that bedroom door was closed a lot. Just seemed normal to us.

That very same day Mom told us to pack up our things so I did. I can't really remember whether Abel and Paul packed their stuff or not. I guess I was in shock. Mom and Dad would spend all day in the bedroom talking. I was scared and didn't know what the hell to do. Late that evening my mom told me to unpack everything. It was not talked about or brought up again ever. I do know my mom starting doing things her way and it was different.

My mother would enroll Abel into a Morris School, a private boys' school just outside of Searcy. Abel was far behind in all his subjects due to being in the hospital so much. I guess it was when I started sixth grade that Mom would decide to put him in a private school. He would continue to go to Morris School until the middle of the eighth grade.

That same year my family would celebrate our first Christmas. The Christmas tree was loaded with gifts. For the first time after going back to school following Christmas break, Abel, Paul and I actually knew what it felt like for all the other kids that had Christmases all those years.

There were many changes and many firsts for myself and my two brothers. Mom would take all three of us on Friday nights and drop us off to go skating or to the movie theatre. She would make sure that there was plenty of money to go to the dairy bar across from the skating rink–plus there were games to play at the skating rink as well. This would continue for a couple of years. I was thirteen now and going into eighth grade. It would only be a matter of months before things would change drastically. I was way ahead of most girls in maturity and puberty. We all know girls mature sooner than boys.

It was 1980, a busy summer for both of my parents. It was also the summer that my mother would find out she was very sick. This was

INFLUENTIAL PAIN

a time when families kept their private life in their home and things did not get talked about outside that door. She did not tell myself or my two brothers that she was sick. I do know she told my older sister, Maureen. I can understand it now but definitely didn't understand it then.

CHAPTER FOUR

IT WAS SUMMER and I had just turned thirteen that past April. That summer in July my mother would have several medical procedures and I would too. I would have my tonsils removed, the birthmark on my right cheek removed and I would get contact lenses. Abel, Paul and myself would also have dentistry work done that was way overdue. Until then, I never gave it a thought why my mother was having all these simple procedures done with me being a teenager and becoming a woman.

I remember it like it was yesterday. The morning I woke up to the desperate voice of my father. He was yelling, " Rebekah, get up!" I ran into the living room to see my Uncle Louis fumbling around through the phone book. Mom was on the couch and Dad was trying to put nitroglycerine underneath her tongue. "Call the ambulance," he yelled. I turned to Uncle Louis and told him Maureen's phone number and to call her. In the middle of all the chaos, I was trying to help my dad put the pill under my mother's tongue. You see she was trying to swallow her tongue. I could see the desperation and panic in my father's eyes. I put a wooden spoon in her mouth to keep her from biting her tongue and Dad's finger. In an instant she threw her left arm up and it was over. I noticed immediately a streak of gray started from the middle of her head of hair all the way to the back of her hairline. Just one streak about two inches wide turned gray right in front of me.

My father looked at me with complete emptiness in his eyes. Then he laid my mom down on the couch. As I helped him, I noticed she had saturated herself. Dad went outside and moved the truck for an ambulance to be able to get in. I just sat there by Mom wondering if it was real.

In a matter of minutes the ambulance would arrive. They had to pick me up and sit me down in the chair. I stood back up and watched as paramedics tried to revive my mom. She was pronounced shortly after 4:00 a.m. The paramedics put her on a gurney, loaded her up, and drove away.

Just a few minutes later my sister would arrive. Behind my sister was Mr. Brigham, who worked for my father. Mr. Brigham was my father's foreman or second boss more or less. Mr. Brigham came over and hugged me really tight. He began cooking me a fried egg and I immediately got sick from the smell and ran down the hallway to the bathroom and started vomiting. I would be sick all day. This day will never leave my mind. Tuesday, November 4th, 1980. It was also election day and one of the longest days of my life—a day of silence and mass confusion for me. I just wasn't able to process it all. I was only thirteen. How does such an innocent mind handle something so damaging that leaves such a permanent mark on the heart, mind and soul? It was the first death I had ever dealt with in my life. I had never been to a funeral or a funeral home. I had no idea what was going on. I do remember it was the worst pain I'd ever felt and I also felt confused, lost and didn't have a damn clue to what was going on and what to do.

As time started passing that morning and during the day, I could only hear several different voices…people talking and me not understanding a word. I was in my room all day trying to understand what had happened that morning. I could not comprehend it or process the reality of my mother's death. I would only leave to go to the bathroom when I got sick but I could see people and food covered the table. A mass of mumbling voices just sounded like an echo in my head. I'm not sure what I was feeling. I only knew I wanted it all to go away.

My dad opened the door around 5:30 to tell me to be ready to go because we would all be going to the funeral home. I began to cry. I

CHAPTER FOUR

was scared. I had no idea what to expect. Seemed like it was forever before 5:30 came around.

When I came out of my room I had no idea what was going on. There were people everywhere: family members, friends and people who I could not even recognize. Someone would come up to me, hug me and tell me, "If there's anything I can do to help just let me know," or they would say, "I'm so sorry, Rachel, I thought the world of your mom or it would be "I loved your mom she was a great person."

I saw my Uncle James, who is a younger brother to my father, so I started trying to make my way over to him because he was my favorite uncle. After several people hugged me and repeatedly said the same thing over and over I finally made it to Uncle James and outside is where we went.

Finally 5:30 p.m. would come. Abel and Paul acted normal as they would do on a daily basis. I'm not sure that they really had grasped onto what happened or were just too immature to understand.

As we loaded up to go to the funeral home I was nervous, scared and didn't have a clue what to expect. I rode with Uncle James and a few other people that I don't remember. There were cars in front of us and behind us. It only made me that much more anxious, wondering what it was going to be like. I had never been to a funeral home nor a funeral. I was, needless to say, terrified. There were a thousand thoughts running through my mind and I didn't like any of them.

Uncle James pulled up to park and it was just a few parking spaces down from the entrance door. Family and friends were standing everywhere. Some had already started going inside and some had not. Uncle James stood beside me and people stared, hugging me and crying. I was really scared and began to cry before Uncle James and I even went inside.

There was a podium stand to the left where a book lay for everyone to sign before going into the viewing area. I remembered there was also a stand and visitor book at home. I signed the book, which felt very awkward to me. Patsy Anna Whiting was at the

INFLUENTIAL PAIN

top of the page with her birthday and death date underneath her name. I just stood there and looked at the book. Before I knew it I was glancing over names that were on it. I'm not sure if I knew these people or remembered them in any way. It was just a lot of signatures to me.

As Uncle James and I began down the hallway, on the left was a big opening to walk through, a casket up front and chairs around the room. The room was filled with flowers everywhere. As I stood and looked, it seemed as though I had tunnel vision; and the tunnel was long, dark and dreary. We began to walk forward. The closer I got, the more frightened I became. As I got there beside her casket I began to get sick. I just stood there and looked. I had nothing to say so Uncle James just stood there holding onto me. My mind was completely blank. I didn't know what to do. I'm not even sure what I was feeling at that moment. This was it. I knew I would never hear my mother's voice again. She was dressed in her favorite color; I guess she looked pretty. All I could do was just stand there feeling lost.

So many emotions revolved regarding what happened that morning. People kept coming up and looking. They would say, "She looks so good."

I just kept thinking she's gone, no more seeing her, nor would I ever hear her voice again. With no one to lead the way I must have stood there for two hours. Not one word could I say. Uncle James said, "Sweetheart, they are about to close. We have to go."

I turned and walked away without saying a word. All I could think about on the way home was her there at that funeral home all alone. Our house was not a home anymore and wouldn't be a home ever again. I was up all night worried about my mother being somewhere else, knowing this was how it was going to be from now on. I kept asking myself why and thinking of all the things I'd never get to tell my mom. I felt so empty, lost, and broken. All I wanted right then was my momma.

Turning and walking away was one of the hardest things I had

CHAPTER FOUR

ever done. All I could think about was Mom being up there in an empty building all alone and in the dark by herself. The next two days would seem to drag on forever. A lot of people would be in and out during this time. There were a lot of family members I would meet that I had never met before. The tears dropped from my cheeks with each hug that they shared with me. My eyes began to swell from so much crying. As the day ended, the house became empty and darkness crept in.

It was Friday, November 7th, the day of the funeral. The final goodbye. The morning seemed to linger on. We would be leaving at 1:00 p.m. and the funeral would start at 2:00. Everyone was beginning to form a line of vehicles. I was behind my father, sister and brother-in-law. I don't remember who I was with except my Uncle James. We arrived at the church. The church was filled with family and friends. As I walked down the aisle I could feel eyes upon me. We finally made it to the first pew. I do not know where any of family members were sitting. I know Uncle James was on my left but I do not know who was on my right side. I just know Dad, brothers and flowers, wreaths and plants filled the church til there was not enough room for all of them. I took a single rose with me.

As services began I was feeling numb and incoherent to what was going on. Then it was time for the family to walk up to say our final goodbyes. I just stood there, Dad was in front of me, and Uncle James was right behind me. Dad stopped for a moment and then walked away. The final viewing was on the way out of the church. I stopped and looked knowing this was the last I would ever see her again. I bent over gave her a kiss and laid the single red rose across her chest.

As I walked out the door I was amazed at the people. I would find out later there were over five hundred people from all walks of life, all creeds and many different ages. This would be an amazing day for my mom, but for me it was a day that would change the dynamics of my family's life forever. Nothing would be normal or the same again. One promise I would make and keep was to always remember her

INFLUENTIAL PAIN

and think of her every day. I kept my promise. I would miss her more and more each passing day. I could only begin to imagine the grief that I'd endure and the road it would take me down. This was only the beginning of all the pain to come.

CHAPTER FIVE

THE NEXT FIVE months would be long, made longer by unbearable loneliness. My dad began to sink himself into grief alongside a bottle of Olde Bourbon. I had to take on extra responsibilities between school, preparing dinner, working on the minnow farm and all the housework. I also took over the paperwork that had to be done. I even handled Dad's personal checking account that paid our bills monthly. I watched my dad dive into the bottle with grief until he made himself sick. I stayed up a lot of nights helping him as he crawled from the bed to the bathroom to vomit. I would wash his face. This lasted a short period of time; then he realized he had to eat and sleep to keep from becoming sick. I'm not sure, but I think he went to the local doctor in Hazen. My father then began to start eating a small lunch and dinner. No matter what, he would steadily drink his "toddy', as he would call it. I knew all too well how to make one for him. My father then started getting up early and going to the minnow shop at 4:00 a.m. and staying there until 9:00 p.m. or later. I usually saw him at dinner.

    Dad grew apart from us when we needed him the most. He didn't realize that he needed us too. Dad grew apart from my younger brother, Paul, and me as well. Abel being sick, Dad was a little more overprotective of him. There was extra work on my end to cover for Paul who liked to goof off most of the time. My days went the same, same routine, hard work, school and no play. Dad began to look at life through the bottom of a bourbon glass so he could never see

INFLUENTIAL PAIN

things clearly or the way things really were. He kept to himself. I never had to ask what needed to be done--I knew. He expected it and that wasn't about to change. I was just hoping that he'd stop drinking and grieving long enough to observe what affect it was having on his children. Somehow, the boys seemed to adjust to everything and handled it a lot better than I could. I knew what work had to be done and I knew my dad was a time bomb waiting to explode. I was just hoping I and my brothers wouldn't be around when it happened.

It wasn't long before I realized that my siblings and I were pretty much on our own. Dad was in no shape to deal with anything. He was so sunk into his pain he couldn't see mine or the suffering I was enduring because of his actions and the way he chose to deal with his pain. As far as I was concerned he had turned his back on his kids who could've pulled him through this and brought some happiness to his life. I would try to tell him it would be okay, knowing it never would be for me or any of us.

While he was trying to escape reality, I was trying to deal with it and help keep the family held together. I had no choice. He was unable to focus himself or us for that matter. I was too young to handle a job that was meant for an adult to carry on their shoulders, not a thirteen-year-old who was trying to be mom and dad. This was a mountainous task but somehow I managed to do the best with what knowledge I had at that age and the responsibilities I was capable of handling.

My dad would become bitter and cold on the inside. My younger brother, Paul, would suffer the repercussions for things that weren't even his fault. Neither Paul nor I would have any idea of what was going on. The damage stuck with me. Paul is still fighting his battle with those demons that were created within our father. He is bitter and cold toward Dad. Paul would not acknowledge him as his dad. Paul will tell you, "Dad hated me and I have no idea why." Paul has let the family know that Dad is not his father as far as he is concerned. Paul definitely doesn't want to be acknowledged as his son. Abel and I had to promise Paul that we would not bury his body anywhere near

CHAPTER FIVE

Dad's grave. When Dad finally passed away, my sister and I got extra plots because my grandfather on my mother's side had already had plots for their family. My mother was buried next to my grandmother, Violet Treadway. The least Maureen and I could do was get enough plots so this family of siblings would be together.

What was amazing about my father is that he only had a fifth grade education. He could read, was very business-oriented and was very intelligent. You would've thought that he had a college degree. He was very educated but an education that he taught himself on his own. When mom passed, all that he was went with her. Now I do not blame him and I'm not bitter. I did not feel this way until I was about twenty-three years old.

Before Dad passed I spent a lot more time with him. I was twenty-five when he told me loved me and was sorry for everything that had happened. By this time he was sick and his time was limited. It would only be a matter of months before he would pass. There were a lot of things we got to talk about during that time. There are also things he told me that no one knows about. I cannot change what happened or take back the things that occurred. I know he was capable of handling things differently than he did. It wasn't the right way to handle it but I can't change that because I'm not Dad. I only hope that Paul will someday overcome the bitterness that's held within. Paul doesn't understand that he's only treating the family the same way Dad did. Paul must learn to forgive in order to be able to move past this point. Otherwise he'll be just like Dad: lonely, cold and bitter…a lonely place where no one wants to be.

I've had my own demons to deal with because of this learned behavior. I sought professional help and have turned my life completely around. I would spend seventeen years of my life being confused over what I went through. I will not pass it on through my children nor will I spend anymore time being unhappy. It took its toll on me. I was very insecure, which led to insecure marriages and divorces, and abusive relationships. This trait was created by my father–then became normal to me. I knew this was something that I did not want

INFLUENTIAL PAIN

carried throughout my generation and those in the future.

I had to be the one to make the decision for myself and my family. I wanted my children to have in life what I was unable to have in my own childhood: peace, stability and a loving home. What a difference the change has made for me and my children. It takes too much energy to hate. Life is too short to hold grudges when it can easily be replaced with happiness. The fulfillment that your children offer in your life will be complete within yourself and within your children.

CHAPTER SIX

JUST OUT OF the blue one day, my dad came to bedroom door and said, "Follow me to the bedroom." He had decided it was time to go through the file cabinet. Dad asked me to help. "I asked Dad, "What exactly are we going to be doing?"

He answered, "Going to look at the letters your momma left for you and your sister and Aunt Ruthy," one of her sisters. He also mentioned she had left a will. Chills just ran down my spine knowing that she had left me a letter. My letter was several pages long and private, not something I will be sharing with anyone.

My father and I started looking over the will. My mother had left one acre of land to each of us five kids. Her car and truck belonged to us five kids including the house we were currently living in. I couldn't fathom it all. My dad had signed and agreed to everything. I now knew exactly what and why my mother did this. She knew my dad would end up drinking and would not take care of legalities so she made sure it was done.

I found it to be very strange the letter she would leave for my father. I understood everything she'd written in his letter but I was perplexed at the fact that she'd actually tell my dad who she wanted him to marry and help finish raising myself, Abel and Paul. As I grew older and became a mother, then and only then did I understand why. In my eyes it takes a very strong woman to choose someone to raise your children. I can't even imagine what she was thinking after finding out she was sick. Now all the things she did before she passed

INFLUENTIAL PAIN

away finally made perfect sense.

My mother had a best friend named Gloria. That was who she chose and all three of us liked Ms. Gloria. My mother stated clearly that she wanted my father to move on. She would write in the letter that Gloria would be the perfect person for him and all of us children. My mother felt like she would be good to us and treat us as if we were her own children. I can remember Gloria and her children coming down and spending a week at a time with mom and the family.

It was the following February after mom's death in November of 1980 when my father decided he would call Gloria. I just remember waking up the next morning and Gloria was there. My father had gone during the night to Pine Bluff and picked her up and any personal belongings she wanted to bring. I do remember the family being happy and we didn't feel so empty anymore.

Gloria tried it for a couple of weeks. I thought everything was going well considering all that had happened. I know that I felt relieved. It seemed like Dad was even feeling more up to his old self again. He had lightened up on the drinking and started spending more time at home. He would come in earlier than before and seemed to be in a happier mood.

My dad always left at about 4:00 a.m. in the morning, which was not abnormal, because most of his customers had minnows to haul somewhere around the state or out of state so they had to load early in order to leave the minnow shop around 5:00 a.m. or by 6:00 a.m. Everyone in our family either on dad's side or my mom's side seemed to be in the minnow business. It was something very common where we lived. People fished and hunted during my years of growing. The new generation doesn't do much of either. Seems as if no one will slow down long enough to enjoy the simple things in life.

Gloria stayed a couple of weeks, then one day she and dad were in the bedroom talking with the door shut as always. I just remember when Gloria came out of the bedroom she'd been crying. I could tell by looking. She tried to act like everything was fine. She would ask Abel, Paul and myself to come sit with her on the couch. She told

CHAPTER SIX

us she was going back home. She began to cry and apologize. I got upset because I knew how it was going to be when she did leave. I hugged her and told her I loved her. I can remember Gloria telling me, "Rebekah, I feel like I'm betraying my best friend, your mother, and I can't live with that." At the time I didn't understand but now, being an adult, I completely understand.

CHAPTER SEVEN

IT WOULDN'T BE long, about two weeks before another woman became a part of our lives. Maureen had run into Nan in the town of Des Arc. Nan would also be my mother's third cousin. She wasn't very pleasant but my father wasn't either. My father would have Maureen get in contact with Nan. Nan appeared at first to be nice. She used all three of us kids by being nice or doing things for us. I guess Dad got to thinking that we needed a mother or a babysitter. At our age we did not need either; we needed our father to be a father. He blamed mother's death on Abel, Paul and me, said we kept Mom stressed out. He was back on the bourbon, as if he had ever quit drinking. I should say my father woke up drinking and went to bed with a glass beside him. Do you have any idea what that did to a mind of thirteen-year-old girl starting to become a young woman?

It would be my dad's fault that Nan would end up moving in. My father had Maureen to find out where Nan lived. Being in a small town everyone knows everyone or think they do. It wasn't long, one week or less, and Nan was moving in. I feel like that was something Dad should have discussed with Abel, Paul and myself. After all, we had already been through enough. Dad was a grown man and made his decisions without consideration of others. His opinion was always right even when he was wrong. This decision would be one that would cost Paul and myself dearly. The price would be greater than he would ever realize.

Nan wasn't dumb, she knew exactly what she was doing. She

CHAPTER SEVEN

caught Dad when he was very vulnerable and under the influence of alcohol. Nan did all the right things as far as my father could see. Nan put up a big front for his kids and my father. At least now he could drink himself to death and choose to be numb about what was going on around him. It's a shame that his own children were worth so little. What my father didn't understand and could've cared less about was the fact that no other woman would ever fill the hole that my mother's death left in my heart. What we needed was our dad and his love. I, myself, was unstable, confused and very trusting of people. I was alone and needed to know there was a stability and security within my safe place. This he could not give and didn't care about anyone but himself at this point. I was broken and fragile to what was coming next.

You don't just move a woman and her four children into your home and say, "Here you go, good luck. You're in charge; see you later." But that's exactly what he had done. This woman came with a package of her own. Nan had four daughters ranging from four years old up to eleven years, all girls. Nan would tell my father her landlord was raising the rent and she couldn't afford her home. She would have to move. Nan at this time received a social security check on four girls from one marriage to a man and only one child actually belonged to him. Nan's deceased husband worked for the railroad so she also received a pension check every month from that company. Nan was bringing an income of $1400 a month in 1981. That was a better income than most people made working forty hours a week. Trust me she was never employed and couldn't read or write. Nan also had a speech impediment. Nan had a car. It was a little older than my mother's but it was hers and I saw nothing wrong with it. But it wouldn't be long before she was driving my mother's car.

My father, Abel, Paul and myself lived in a three bedroom mobile home. I was wondering how we were all going to fit into this small home. It was a nice mobile home and brand new when we moved into it--our home may have been around eight years old at the time.

INFLUENTIAL PAIN

After Nan moved in she immediately began playing her role. She took over in no time. A woman who had nothing began to take advantage of everything. Nan began wearing my mother's clothes. My mother's personal jewelry box was left to me, Nan ended up with it and the jewelry. The hurt just grew into deeper hurt and pain. Soon as we all know, hurt and pain will eventually turn into hatred when you have a father allowing it to happen. This was only the beginning of the pain and hurt that I would endure from a woman that was evil and selfish. The price was great and costly in many ways, mentally and emotionally. Nan's daughters also benefitted well at my expense.

My parents weren't considered poor at this time. Both of my parents had stable businesses, were well to do, and had acquired a lump sum of money. Nan knew this and took complete advantage of this opportunity. Nan made sure my father never ran out of Olde Bourbon. She would buy half gallons by the case. The more he drank the less he could see what was going on around him nor did he give a shit anyway. Nan wanted my father blind to what was going on and she succeeded in all her plans. By this time I had grown scared of what was going to happen next. Nan told lie after lie. My brother, Paul, endured beatings and I would endure all the housework, cooking, helping her daughters with their homework, etc.

As each day passed and I would get off the bus, my fear only grew daily. I would have no idea what I was going to be walking into when I came into the house. Fear and dread of that bus ride home can never be put into words. Unless you have lived it you just wouldn't understand. I was already afraid of and wouldn't dare cross those boundaries that he had set so many years ago. There was no way I would do anything to get into trouble. The consequences with Dad were not ones you wanted to pay. He was physical with his punishment. This would leave marks and scars on the body and heart of a young teenager who could not understand. I also could never comprehend why my father wouldn't ask myself or Paul what happened. He took Nan's word and we lost our right to speak and to be heard. Paul would take both hands and grab the back of his head when he walked through

CHAPTER SEVEN

the doorway and would run to his and Abel's bedroom. I can't even imagine the fear he felt doing this every day. Fear is not a good feeling and not an atmosphere you want to live in daily. It became a part of life for me and Paul, something that created an anxiety disorder for the both of us.

CHAPTER EIGHT

NOW LET'S TALK about Nan's daily routine so you understand everything. Nan always seemed to have a reason for needing to run down to DeValls Bluff to see her family and share my parents' wealth. She was always giving them money behind my father's back and buying things for her family. Nan's family was very poor and I knew that. She managed to spend her days away from the house so when I came in from school all the work was left for me to do. I always had to cook supper for nine people which took at least three hours between cooking and cleaning the kitchen up. Imagine cooking for one family and now having to cook for two families. It took pans of fried chicken and two pans of fried potatoes and usually five to six cans of vegetables (always two vegetables). Then when everyone was finished, my second line of work would begin.

I had to help Nan's three youngest daughters with their homework and get them bathed and ready for bed. After I finished all of my work I then had my own homework and bath to get done. I would get in bed about 11:00 p.m. and start all over again around 4:00 a.m. I'd get myself ready for school, then get her girls up and ready for school. That meant feeding them breakfast, washing those dishes and watching for the bus. We lived in the country so we would catch the bus around 6:45 a.m.

After about a month the house was full. Abel and Paul had their own bedroom to share being the only boys. Before, I had my own room. Now I had to sleep with Nan's oldest daughter and the three

CHAPTER EIGHT

younger ones were on pallets on the floor. I guess Nan evidently didn't like those accommodations for her daughters. Nan's daughters wanted their own rooms. Nan and my father would come up with a solution. I came in from school one day and there was a new storage building outside. Those silver tin metal ones. My father would insulate and put paneling on the walls. He would then run electricity to it for lights.

I was wondering what the new building was for, when I found out I was astonished that Dad would even consider and approve of this decision. I ended up with a twin bed and one chest of drawers for my clothes and a wooden rod for my other clothes. My new bedroom. I was booted out of the house into a building. My thoughts were: Nan is getting her way with everything and how could I mean so little to put me in a primitive building? This is when I started experiencing emotional problems. I kept on going like everything was normal and never told a soul. I knew it wouldn't have made a difference. I had no choice and wasn't given a choice. I would move my things into this building. I didn't get any of the bedroom furniture my mother had gotten me. That meant more to me than anything and just broke my heart.

It took a little bit of getting used to. I was sleeping outside in a building that made me feel scared and unsafe. I would hear every little noise. Everything you could imagine ran through my mind. I was always afraid that someone would break in thinking that there was something valuable stored up. It seemed to take forever to fall asleep. It seemed like I wasn't asleep long before the alarm would go off and it was time to start another day. I finally decided one day to decorate my new bedroom, so maybe I would feel more comfortable or maybe let some of who I was out. I created a calm and soothing atmosphere, totally different than what my life was really like.

My father never took Abel back to the doctor after mother passed away. He would have a three wheeler accident with my cousin that would actually save his life. Abel and my cousin were riding separate three wheelers. My cousin's wheel puncturede Abel's rear tire and he

INFLUENTIAL PAIN

ended up snagging his leg into the wheel and broke his leg in four different places, tearing the flesh to the bone. He would have four metal pins in his leg for about six months.

This accident was a blessing in disguise because Abel was already dying from kidney poison and never knew it. The doctor was furious with my father and explained he would not have lived another two weeks and now Abel would need a kidney transplant due to not having medical care for almost three years.

I began to use this place as my safe haven and an escape from everyone else and all the ugly things going on around me. I cried a lot when I was alone and wondered what I had done to deserve all that I was getting. I somehow managed to stay busy to keep me strong but on the inside I was crushed, broken into, and lost without any direction or encouragement. I was alone and very lonely. I wasn't able to spend nights with friends or they weren't able to spend the night with me. My neighbor, Betty, was about three years older than me. She was the only friend I had and the only place I could stay overnight. This routine remained the same for almost three years. During those three years things would only get worse. Paul, my younger brother, and I were alone with the abuse. It was about three weeks before I turned sixteen that something happened that would change my life.

CHAPTER NINE

THE DAY THAT started it all off was the morning when my father had overstepped his boundaries. I remember this morning very well. I was standing in the kitchen in front of the sink and Nan said, "I tried to tell Paul but he always has a smart ass mouth." I was full of rage. I could hear Paul screaming in the background. I went into the bedroom and my father was beating him with a two by four. I said, "I've had enough." I turned around and walked into my father's gun cabinet, grabbed the shot gun, returned to the bedroom, and opened the door. "Hit him just one more time and I'm going to blow your fucking head off." My father dropped that two by four and left. I walked through the kitchen and told Nan, "You're next, bitch."

I returned to the bedroom and Paul was soaked in blood across his back and buttocks. I didn't know what to do except get him cleaned up, on the bus and out of the house. Paul skipped school that day. He was worried that Coach Fulton would make him dress out for P.E. and he couldn't let anyone see.

I remember that day all too well. I was a sophomore and was sitting in literature class. The teacher was going over notes that we had taken in order to prepare for a test. I was listening but not looking at my notes. Out of nowhere I just fell apart and started crying. My teacher talked to me after class. I didn't say much. I didn't have to. I didn't realize she also had a degree in phycology. I just gave her a few small details about what was going on in my home. She asked me who I could call that would help. I only knew my brother-in-law,

INFLUENTIAL PAIN

Lynn, and she would get that number from me. I do know she called Lynn and I remember the conversation the two had over the phone. I'm keeping that private and my teacher's name private. One point she stressed to Lynn very clearly, "You must get Rebekah out this house before she commits suicide." I had never once thought about suicide because I felt responsible for my two brothers. This was a time when DHS didn't exist. If so, maybe I would have gotten the help I needed to make things different. It was in a time when people didn't get involved with what went on under someone else's roof.

I would find out later that Mrs. Petray had a degree in psychology and that made her more aware of what was going on. I would find out also years later that she told Maureen I would have committed suicide if I didn't get away from this atmosphere. I'm not sure I would've ever done such a thing, just not my nature. I only know I am here today to tell my story.

That afternoon after school I got off the bus and my sister's vehicle was there. I got inside only to see Lynn there as well. Lynn was doing all the talking. "I'm here to pick up Rebekah and there's not a damn thing you're going to do about it."

I was speechless. No one ever talked to my father that way. I got a few clothes and we all three left.

It was a couple of months later or less, that my older brother, Albert, went and got Paul and he would stay with Maureen and Lynn also. Paul was in a very emotional state of mind. My sister and I tried everything to help, but it was impossible. Paul was bitter, filled with hatred and very lost. It had gotten to a point in which Maureen and myself did not know what to do to help. Together we would talk to Paul and he had very good and dear friends, Brooks and Dana, and they would take him. It made a big change in his life at this time.

CHAPTER TEN

MAUREEN WOULD MAKE it a point that my sixteenth birthday was a special one. I had just moved to Hazen and been in school for about two weeks, waiting on my scores from a correspondence course I had taken. I didn't know many people and hadn't acquired many friends.

Lynn was a mechanic and well known around Hazen. A lot of high school boys came by frequently to get their vehicles worked on or looked at. Lynn would invite them to the party and have them spread the word around. I invited just a few girls that I knew. It turned out better than I thought it would. It felt good to not be alone anymore for the first time in a very long time.

I would meet a guy at my birthday party. I was actually a friend of his sister. Lauren was the first girl at Hazen School to talk to me and become my friend and that friendship continues today. Lauren's brother's name was Greg. We would start dating and dated through the rest of his school year. Greg was in a private school, Subiaco, for boys only. Greg came home on the weekends and I would also go up to see him when possible. It was Greg's senior year and I walked in the homecoming and his sister, Lauren, would as well.

I grew close to Greg and depended on him. For the first time in a long time I felt safe. I had someone I could talk to whom I knew wouldn't judge me. Greg made me feel loved and safe. I was still a virgin, something I planned to remain until I married. I was a little over seventeen years old and Greg was almost nineteen and was growing impatient. I was just plain scared. I knew nothing about sex.

INFLUENTIAL PAIN

Greg was also a virgin, at least that's what he told me. I tried to be understanding of his feelings and I didn't know who to talk to about it because I was feeling embarrassed and scared at the same time. Finally I talked to my sister, Maureen, about it and decided to get on birth control first. I only knew I didn't want to do anything I felt uncomfortable with or wasn't ready for.

I thought about it for awhile and finally decided I was ready. Looking back now, I don't believe I was ready at all. The first experience wasn't pleasant for me. I wasn't willing to do that again for another three months. I dreaded it because it was painful and what you hear from girls I found out wasn't true at all. I would have preferred to be told it hurts the first time and will for a few times.

I took my birth control every day. It would take a trip to doctor to see how everything was going, only to find out I was six weeks pregnant. I'm thinking how was this possible after being on birth control? I just sat down and cried. I had no clue what I was going to do. It changed everything. Greg was in the middle of his year at college and it wasn't what we had planned. I had no clue how I was going to tell him, knowing this changed everything. He was Catholic and their beliefs were only making it more difficult. I knew his parents would be pissed and with reason to be.

I was just trying to figure out how to approach this subject with Greg, knowing that it was going to change what he had planned. It wasn't the end of the world but it sure felt like it was. I kept the pregnancy to myself for a week or so trying to decide how to handle it and trying to understand myself that I was actually pregnant yet wasn't ready for children. It not only affected Greg's future but mine as well. We were just beginning to enjoy the fact of being out of school and working our way to the future we had talked about. We'd only discussed what we wanted to do with our lives as far as jobs and future retirement. Not once had Greg and I ever talked about marriage. I guess we just knew that's what was in the future and when the time was right we would make decisions then.

It was December of 1984 that Greg and I would get married. Greg

CHAPTER TEN

being Catholic, we felt like it was the right thing to do. There were going to be issues because of his Catholicism. Greg talked to the priest and he agreed to marry us. It was a large wedding. Catholics believe in large weddings and a big party afterwards. There were around five hundred at the wedding. It was lovely. One thing for sure, Greg and I both gave up our dreams to do what we thought was right at the time.

Greg would leave college and we'd move to Little Rock in order to find jobs. Greg worked a warehouse where he loaded trucks to deliver food products. Myself, I found a job babysitting a toddler that paid fifty dollars a week. It was best since I was pregnant and waiting on tables was not ideal. We managed very well and then Greg decided he wanted to start taking over his dad's business and work for him. I was okay with that because I would be around family and not so lonely since Greg worked nights and I babysat during the day. We didn't see each other much.

Around April of 1985 we moved to Slovak so Greg could start working for his dad and get ready to go out of state for work. Greg's dad owned a seed cleaning business. We rented a house in Slovak. I loved the house. It had three bedrooms and a freezer room and laundry room off the carport. I guess it wasn't long before Greg would go out of state and would just get everything ready for the baby we were about to have. I stayed sick a lot throughout my pregnancy. I don't know why they call it morning sickness. I was sick all the damn time.

Greg's mother, Mrs. Thelma, would make sure I had a baby shower. Mrs. Thelma and the women from church got together and gave me a wonderful baby shower. I had everything imaginable for a baby. I actually began to look forward to our future. Everything seemed so right: stability, nice home and a good business for a bright future. I would soon find out that things aren't always as they seem. Putting all of your trust in someone is a good thing; just make sure it's the right person. Never assume or take anything for granted.

I decided to invite my cousin, Sherri, and her husband, Rex down for the weekend since Greg was working out of state and the due date was getting close. Funny how things work out. I woke up during the

INFLUENTIAL PAIN

early hours of the morning and went to the bathroom and my water broke. I yelled at Sherri and we were three people running around in a hurry. Rex turned the flashers on and away we went. I would deliver pretty quickly and Greg made it in from Oklahoma that evening around 4:00 p.m.

This beautiful little girl entered our lives at 10:24 a.m. and three weeks early at that. She would weigh four pounds and twelve ounces. I was told by the doctor that she was healthy—just needed to get to five pounds and we could go home. Two days later my daughter, Carrie, and I would go home.

As far as I knew everything was going well. Greg would come home every couple weeks for the weekend and once in awhile a week at a time. I totally trusted him with every fibre of my being. Three months passed and I was going back to work. Carrie's grandma, Thelma, would keep Carrie while I worked and I would pick her up when I got off work. I got off work early one night and ended up with the surprise of my life.

I stopped by the house to let Greg know I had gotten off work early before I picked up Carrie. I walked in the doorway off the garage, entering the kitchen. I could hear the TV on but no one was in the living room. I started down the hall and next thing I know Greg and another woman came out of the bedroom and all hell broke loose. Things happened so fast I couldn't even begin to tell you what happened partly because some things are just personal. Needless to say I left to go pick up Carrie and when I got back she was gone.

I cried. I was so shocked, hurt, and speechless. I was overwhelmed. I did not believe in cheating. I would find out this had been going on for quite some time. My daughter was three months old and this girl was five months pregnant with Greg's child. So I packed our things, rented another home and got divorced. No returning, no working it out. The only person I had in the world, crushed my world.

After that my opinion of men was not a good one. So I began to live for myself and wasn't going to let any guy get to me again. When I met Greg, there was a wall around my heart. I could not even tell him

CHAPTER TEN

all that I had been through. So I put all those bad things in the back of my mind and acted like it never existed. In all honesty I did not share myself completely with him. It hurt for a while but not long. It wasn't long at all before he was put in the back of my mind and didn't exist. We had very little contact with each other and he would remarry very quickly after our divorce (and not the girl he impregnated). I was not bothered because there were no longer any feelings for this man.

I would meet someone else about three years later. At first he was a pest and I did not have any interest in him. He would just keep coming back and irritating me more, so finally I gave in and went out with him. I had no control over my feelings for this man but I did fall in love with him. It was different than being with Greg...a different kind of love. True love for the very first time. I lived with him about a year. Then he asked me to marry him and I turned him down.

I thought things were great. He was well known around the small town we lived in and his family was well to do. He worked all the time. I worked at the local restaurant as I did when we met. He just seemed to never get home until 8:00 or 9:00 p.m. every night. At first I just thought he was a workaholic because in some sense he was, just like his dad. He was working hard all right, at cheating. I wasn't going through that again. I began to wonder what was wrong these men or what was wrong with me?

This time the pain and hurting would last. I felt like it was never going to end. I just couldn't handle it so I chose to move to Little Rock. It took eight years to get over this man. I have no regrets, I felt love, knew what it was, and I also knew what real hurt was. I decided after that I would never get close enough to ever feel that way again and I kept my word. That was a love that filled my heart, my soul and my mind. I was doubtful that I would ever find it again. Honestly, I didn't want to find it again. The one and only time I wanted to go through that. I'm a quick learner and now nurtured a hardened heart toward men.

CHAPTER ELEVEN

IT WASN'T LONG before I created a pattern for myself that would lead me through two marriages: no stability and plenty of drama and domestic violence–relationships that would change my life forever. This pattern I chose created nothing but pain and fear. I felt like I was about to lose my mind. I would go back to the atmosphere that my dad created for me. It would be my safe haven, my normal. How crazy does that sound? Learn what you live and live what you learn.

I chose men that I would like but knew I couldn't love. I would be like my father in some sense. No emotions and no remorse. I was able to choose men that would be abusive and wanted to stay in that relationship. I guess I was used to it or maybe felt like that's just the way it was no matter whom or whatever. So I chose to keep to myself, wrapped and trapped by these types of men. After about six months I would be tired of one guy and would move on to someone else but never in a hurry. That would go on until I reached bottom at the age of thirty-two years old.

I needed a change. I was still hurting and it was time to move from a small town of getting nowhere to a town with more options to move up the ladder, or so I thought. A friend of my mother's was the manager of a restaurant in Little Rock. I went to her and got a job. I started two days later. The money was good and the business was good. I worked from 5:00 a.m. to 2:00 p.m. I lived forty five minutes away. It was a good drive but worth it.

CHAPTER ELEVEN

I had to come a point in my life in which it was time to move and I wasn't dating much. Between having my daughter and working early shift, I was so tired and I went to bed by 7:00 p.m. I found an apartment in North Little Rock. Nice little two bedroom apartment at the right price with easy access to the interstate to work. Living in a bigger city took some getting used to but I definitely loved the conveniences and choices of things to do. When you're younger you can adapt easier.

After about two or three months of working there I met a man who was also a manager at the same place, just a different department. I hadn't dated in a while and he asked me out to dinner and I thought, why not? I would see him from time to time in the waitress station getting a drink but he never spoke. My understanding from my boss was that he had been a manager over his department for about ten years. He was chief engineer.

Terry and I would continue to date. We had a lot of fun together. Terry seemed to like kids and got along fine with my daughter as far as I could tell. We would date about six months and he brought up the idea of maybe living together. I thought why not? give it a try. So Terry moved in with me. Before I knew it, another six months had passed by. Finally one day out of the blue he brought up marriage. Terry had been married before for five years and no children. We would talk about it off and on for about a week and then I said yes. This marriage would change me, my life, my daughter's life and do more damage than good. It would change my life forever in ways I would have never imagined.

CHAPTER TWELVE

THE FIRST TWO or three months would be great. Then there was a change. The man I thought I knew, I didn't know at all. It wasn't long before the verbal abuse would begin. Terry had been married previously, married for five years. He had no children that I was aware of. I got along with his friends, they all told me nothing, they thought I was the one who would change him from the person they knew but they were wrong. It was only after he started shoving me around, a slap here and there. I really didn't know what to do. Unfortunately, Terry's friends were dead wrong.

One of Terry's good friends of many years, Jack, would finally tell me about the abuse endured by his first wife. I told Jack, "Abusers don't change; I know, I saw it out of my father." An abuser never changes, he just finds new victims.

It wouldn't be long before the shoving and slapping turned into black eyes, busted lips and broken noses. Bruises that people could see and ones that underneath clothing never got seen. I started like most women, making excuses and kept on working.

We were married two years and I decided to leave. He wouldn't have it. Terry would never leave me alone. Terry would call and tell me what way I went to work and what my daughter was wearing when I dropped her at school. I never saw Terry anywhere in spite of keeping my eyes always wide open. I couldn't handle it anymore. It was easier living with him than living in fear with him or without him. That fear doesn't outweigh the other.

CHAPTER TWELVE

Terry was unpredictable. I couldn't handle the stalking anymore. I became fearful. Terry was full of threats and was one who followed through with those threats. It just seemed easier to give in but the ugly reality was that I knew I'd be lucky to get out alive.

The domestic violence laws were different then than they are today. I called the police; they were absolutely no help. I felt like I was in a no win situation and in reality I was. I would endure this abuse for another two years. My family couldn't understand why I stayed, as most families don't. They have no idea what fear and control feels like. It came to a point where I didn't see him much and nobody knew what was going on.

I was never able to go to Thanksgiving or Christmas with my family. You see, an abuser shuts everyone out. Terry would make sure I had a black eye or was bruised up so badly that I couldn't go in looking like that, it wasn't allowed anyway. It was a reason for Terry to do what he does best, abuse people. Fear gave him the tool he needed to control the marriage.

Terry made me feel worthless, stupid and made me believe that no one would want me and I believed him. The mind control they have over your mind is what keeps you from leaving. This is the way Terry kept control, There was nothing in our lives which I had any control over. If women weren't terrorized no one would remain in an abusive relationship. Unless you're in this kind of relationship or have been, you're the only ones who truly understand. You feel alone and your partner will make sure you are alone. This is the only Terry who could keep total control.

I was on a routine that Terry created for me, and you follow that routine as long as you're in this relationship. It didn't matter that I did the same thing every day, just the way Terry wanted. Terry always found something wrong. One day it's fine and the next day it's completely wrong. I trained myself to accommodate his needs and I didn't cross those lines, but I did lose who I was in the process.

CHAPTER FOURTEEN

HOW IRONIC THAT my cousin's wife, Angel, would become my best friend. Someone I needed in my life. God sends the right person at the right time. Angel would give me the strength I needed to get through it.

It wouldn't be long until Angel was right. I would get strong enough to leave this man only after he almost took my life. Terry and I lived in a townhouse in North Little Rock. I worked a split shift at a restaurant about four or five blocks away from our home. Our townhouse was very nice, the rich area, we had two patios, one upstairs and one downstairs. You could look out patio doors downstairs and right across the street was Baptist Memorial Hospital. From where we lived it was across the yard and across the street was the E.R. entrance. It was maybe a half block away.

I would come home from work. The restaurant closed at 8:00 p.m. I had to shut down and clean everything up. I also had to wait on any remaining customers. I would sidework to finish before closing as we all do before we leave work.

I arrived home, and it happened to be a Tuesday night. It was about ten minutes after 8:00 p.m. Terry had been drinking and was acting all crazy. I would later find out he was smoking crack. I immediately started cooking dinner. I was making a taco casserole in the skillet. The hamburger meat was cooking. I started dicing up an onion to put in it. He started in on who was I messing around with?

I looked at Terry and said, "You know better than that. I'm not a

CHAPTER FOURTEEN

cheater and don't ever intend on being one, just my belief!!"

Terry kept on, "Who is he?" I turned around and looked at him and said, "What did I say, you know me better than that." I kept on dicing up the onion and Terry kept hounding on this cheating. I still had my work uniform on. My uniform was a t-shirt with the restaurant's logo on it and a skirt below the knees.

The next thing I knew he was in the silverware drawer and pulled out a twelve inch serrated knife. I turned around and looked at him and said, "What are you doing?' He pointed the knife to my face and said, "Who is he?'

I in return said, "I don't know what you're talking about." Before I knew it he had stabbed me. I tried to move but couldn't. He went through the front side of my right inner thigh, all the way through and pinned me to the kitchen cabinet. I told him I couldn't move and he thought I was crazy. Terry grabbed the handle of the knife and jerked it out and when he did it was as if from the front of my skirt torn flesh and blood just started gushing out. I freaked out.

I looked out of the corner of my eye and there was my daughter standing at the bottom of the stairway. She had seen everything. I grabbed several dish towels and started wrapping my thigh and tying a tourniquet. These towels would be soaked in no time. My flesh was hanging out on the outside of my leg. I knew that I needed medical treatment or I was going to bleed to death. Terry just kept saying, "I'm not going to jail." He would keep repeating this over and over.

I just kept thinking *I'm going to die and he's going to kill my daughter. I've got to get her out alive whether I make it or not.* I begged to go to the emergency room and he kept saying no. I told him, "I'll die and sooner or later people are going to be looking for me." He finally gave in after three days, six hours and ten minutes. My daughter had to swear not to talk at all. We all got in his car and around the block we went to the emergency room. Nurses took me back immediately. Terry made my daughter stay up front and not to say a word. Nurses asked me what happened. I told them I was dicing up an onion and there was water on the floor. I had slipped and fallen with the knife in

INFLUENTIAL PAIN

my hand and next thing I knew I had cut my leg. Terry stayed in the room the whole time.

It would take twenty-two stitches on the inside and eighteen stitches on the exit side of my leg. The nurse looked at me and said, "You are lucky to be alive." It lacked less than a quarter inch from severing my femoral artery. By this time my daughter was in the room and I was cleaned and really don't remember what happened in between, including the stitching of my leg. The nurse gave me three prescriptions. That was the longest night ever. I never went to sleep and neither did Terry. I called in sick the next day. Terry called in sick and didn't leave those three days either.

I was just waiting for the opportunity to sneak out or slip away if possible. I fell asleep, only to awaken and sew he wasn't there, or so I thought. I wasted no time. I went upstairs, woke up my daughter, and told her to hold on tightly to my hand. I ran straight to the emergency room. I told the nurses what really happened. Police officers already knew it wasn't an accident. The police arrived and we went back my house and he was gone. I told the police everything that had happened in the past three days. Terry was immediately issued a warrant and arrested.

The prosecuting attorney at the time wanted to make it a big case for the media: newspaper articles and TV coverage and I just couldn't let that happen. I did not want anyone from the small towns knowing and didn't want to get that look every time I ran into someone I knew. We all know how a small town is. Twenty years later and someone is going to see you and say, "There's that girl…."

A few days later I hired an attorney from Stuttgart, who also was the prosecuting attorney for Arkansas County. My attorney was there emotionally and understandingly through this whole process. I got my divorce and knew a trial was awaiting in about ten months. Then came the panic of where to go and what to do to feel safe again.

I would move north of Little Rock and drive for an hour and half to work somewhere southeast of where I lived in hopes of not being found. That would last for about three months and my only open

CHAPTER FOURTEEN

day was Sunday. There were no cell phones then. I had an unlisted number and one Sunday morning my phone rang and I answered and recognized the voice immediately. The only words were, "You can't move or go anywhere that I can't find you." I panicked and moved to Covington, Tennessee for the remainder of time while awaiting trial.

CHAPTER FIFTEEN

IT WOULD BE close to five years before I got involved with someone I knew during my childhood. I had gone out with Ray a couple times after getting out of school and he'd been a senior in Hazen High School. I was crazy about him at that time. Ray was a friend to me and my first husband as we all knew each other and hung out on the weekends at college. I also ran into Ray after my divorce and we went riding around and just hanging out. I would be working in an infamous restaurant when we crossed paths again four years later. Ray had just been through a divorce about year prior to that. His marriage lasted about five years. We caught up on the past and what we had been doing over the last seven years. I never spoke of what happened.

Before we knew it we were in a relationship. We ended up spending time together for about two months and I moved in with Ray. Three months later I would find out I was pregnant. At the time I was happy, everything was going really well. We grew close to each other because we were both damaged goods although we never talked about it.

During the fifth month of my pregnancy I started having complications and ended up at the emergency room. I had been diagnosed with placenta previa and would be spending the remainder of the pregnancy in the hospital.

During this time we would grow really close. Ray was there every morning before he went to work and every afternoon when he got off work. He would visit until about 8:00 pm so he would have an hour

CHAPTER FIFTEEN

drive home and get some rest. I grew very close to him. I depended on him and he was there for me.

On the weekends he would take one day and bring my daughter up to spend the day and take the next day for house cleaning, laundry and taking care of necessary things that needed to be done around the house. My sister-in-law kept my daughter during the week.

I would spend sixty-two days in the hospital before I delivered our first son. Our son would be two months premature and he would spend some time in NICU. After sixty-four days in the hospital I was released. I was more than ready to come home; unfortunately, our son would not be. We were very blessed. Gary's lungs were fully developed, but he was jaundiced and needed blood transfusions after he was born. We only had to wait for his weight gain so he could be released.

Two weeks later our son would be able to come during the Thanksgiving holidays. It wasn't long after this that Ray decided he wanted to get married. I was so hesitant. I thought things were great the way they were. Ray would start saying, "It's not right. He's a bastard child." I finally gave in and said yes.

We would have a private ceremony in our home. I was sick the morning of the wedding. I just felt so uncomfortable for some reason. I would find out way too soon why I had those feelings.

About two weeks into our marriage things started to change drastically. Ray knocked me down on the floor and knocked the breath out of me. I told him I would not live this way—that was simply not going to happen. It would be one month later when I found a job and went to stay with a family member. I guess I stayed about three months. Ray drove me crazy the whole time, so I went back. I stayed for about six months then I filed for divorce.

I then roommated with another female who had a couple of children. It would be Gary's first birthday. My roommate invited Ray to come without my knowledge. When he showed up I started shaking. I had no clue what was going on and why Ray was there. My roommate told me she invited him and I asked why? Why would you do such a thing and not even ask me nor tell me?

INFLUENTIAL PAIN

Ray and I started talking on the phone. He had gotten a better job and moved out of town about an hour and half away. We started spending time together and before I knew it I was right back with him. In two months I would end up pregnant with our second child. I stayed until our son was about two or three months old. Then I couldn't handle it anymore.

Things went well for about one year. There would be no contact with Ray for about thirteen months. This is when I began to notice I had a pattern with these types of men.

I remarried Ray because he drove me crazy and it just seemed easier. I would stay almost a year and finally walk out for good. I had handled all the abuse I could handle. My last go round I ended up in the hospital. There would be a nurse who was around fifty years in age. I never told him what was going on, he just knew. He would be a volunteer for a battered women and children shelter.

He treated me and was going to release me, but he pulled up his stool, looked at me and said, "The last girl I let walk out the door, her husband shot and killed her that night. That night has never left me, would you let me help you? It would be confidential."

I said okay. He then gave me a phone number to a lady who could help. I burned that number into my brain and threw the paper away.

So I made the call the next day. I met her at the hospital and filled out papers for a court order for me and for my children–an order of protection. After Ray was served with this order we went to court. I was a nervous wreck. I had already been down this road for so many years. I was tired. About two weeks later he would break my door down. The police were called and gave him a break because he worked for the state.

About a month later I would need Ms. Carol's help again. This time I was leaving town and staying with a friend that only I knew about. Ms. Carol would meet me and my children a couple blocks from my apartment and take us to my friend's house.

Someone died that day and someone new was reborn. Thank you Mr. Green, nurse, and Ms. Carol.

CHAPTER SIXTEEN

I WOULD HOLD my own for about two years. My oldest daughter ended up back with me. I had to get full custody and custody of an unborn grandchild. I began to notice I was having problems sleeping. Everything I had been through was coming to the surface. I was seeing a doctor and for a year he tried everything to help. Nothing seemed to work. One day I walked into his office and went to the back. I told him "It's time for professional help. He responded, "I was waiting on you to ask, but until you asked, my advice wasn't doing any good.

I would see a psychiatrist and therapist. I was diagnosed with high anxiety disorder and severe concurring depression. Through my primary doctor I was diagnosed with severe chronic GERDs disease. I would vomit all the time due to excessive anxiety and my stomach producing excessive acid due to anxiety.

Now I'm beginning my second anniversary with a therapist and my psychiatrist. Things have changed drastically. I'm working with, not for, two State Senators and I'm strengthening myself as I try to pass one new law against domestic violence.

I am a keynote speaker for Advocate to stop to Domestic Violence. I also take my own personal time to help women get orders of protection and help needed. I also worked with the Coalition Against Domestic Violence and was a board member. I was able to strengthen five laws and pass one new law.

I was the first advocate to have a video made that narrated my

INFLUENTIAL PAIN

story. It was presented at our Annual Amethyst Ball. I would proceed to be an advocate for eighteen years and divorced for twenty-one years.

I had enough strength to make the change for myself and break the cycle my children would have carried on. It's not easy but worth it.

Special thanks to my new psychiatrist, Melanie. Special thanks to my therapist Winter, Licensed Trauma Therapist of a private practice.

The past two and half years have been difficult revising this book and getting it ready for publication. The road was long as was reliving it all over again. I could not have done it without their help.

I'm diagnosed with complex PTSD, and there are days that I think I won't make it to next but I do. Just know that putting all the bad stuff away and keeping it bottled up comes with a cost. Being abused comes with lifetime long term affects.

I am a survivor and there is life beyond abuse. It's not easy but much better.

The life of abuse and the cycle can carry on through generations until someone is strong enough to break the cycle of the family. I was strong enough to break that cycle, but I was older before it would change and I learned what I had to do to make the change. I never abused my children but I did marry two abusive men because of it. The one thing I know, you learn what you live and you live what you learn. This is very true and I've seen it within my family and outside of my family.

QUOTES

These are quotes that I have written during the process of writing my book. They are in order by date as they were written.

September 23, 2005
"When I started writing this book about seven or eight months ago I never realized the changes I would go through. The closet door that had been locked for over twenty years was finally overpacked and was beginning to open on its own. There was no control over keeping the door closed anymore. I had finally hit the bottom. I would feel the pain all over again, it had been buried for so long. I actually had to teach myself to express my feelings. Cry if needed, get angry if needed. It involves exploring another side I've never been able to cross over into. All the emotions that would come out, the restless nights. It's like a roller coaster ride. I'm just waiting for the ride to end. I want to move past this, I want to be happy within. I know that day will come. It took twenty years to take this toll on me and it'll be a long road to full recovery but I've learned that there are two keys to happiness in life. First, be true to yourself and who you are. Second, be happy within yourself and have respect for yourself. I will soon learn how to deal with my own demons and move forward in life and be happy. It's funny something that is supposed to come so naturally in your life now becomes something you must be taught to do. Makes you wonder if true happiness will ever reside inside."

INFLUENTIAL PAIN

INFLUENTIAL PAIN September 29, 2005
"It's amazing how the influence of one person can cause a winding pattern of insecurities. We sometimes do not realize the power an adult can have over a child. It can cause you a life of great pain or create an opposite pattern of success. I guess it depends on the person and what they're capable of handling. Just remember if you're an adult and small eyes are watching, you are their hero, so everything you do or decision you make will have a bearing on the outcome of their lives. So if you suffer from pain, your child will too. What you say or do really does matter. After mom passed all I had was my dad, and even before Mom passed. You know how little girls love their dad. It's a different kind of love from the kind of love that we feel for our mother. I watched a man so tall, dive into grief and pain. He hit bottom and stayed bottomed out. He forgot that he was the hero. Although I had no control over my dad or the way he chose to deal with his pain, he did not understand that I learned to deal with it the same way. So now the winding road begins with the writing of the book "Influential Pain."

October 2, 2005
"It's funny how little things can be taken for granted. For instance, my six-year-old son comes in this morning gives me a hug, I hug him back. I noticed while I'm rubbing his back he is also coaxing me at the same time, by rubbing my arm and back. We tell each other we love each other. As he leaves the room I think about the little things that mean so much are often taken for granted. I always tuck the kids into bed, hug them and tell them I love them. In the morning I wish for them to have a good day at school, etc. I did not actually realize until this morning how special those moments are. Something they'll always remember and carry with them. My parents are so busy with work and their own lives, those little things we did not receive. My mother was more compassionate than my dad. He was hard core and from as they say, "old school." My father was molded into a man that

expected perfection, to explain something once and exhibit no compassion, no hugs and never I love you. On the other hand, Mother was a busy woman. What little time we had with her through the day meant something to her, I hope. I understand that now. I hope that my compassion and love will burn like a flame of hope through my children. What I missed out on when I was child, I want it to overflow within my children. Then one day, as I have done, the moment will hit them. Then I'll know I passed on a forgiving, caring and undying love through my children. This is something they can cherish and remember and bestow in their own children."

October 7, 2005
Love is a funny thing. We all believe more than one time that we're in love with someone. It's only when things don't work out that you actually realize how you feel. So how do you ever really know when it's the right one? So many times we think this is the one, then it's not, so how do you know? It's funny how the older generation says you'll know when it happens, then when that moment happens will you know, will you be able to grasp onto what you feel or what you think you might feel? Most people know when it's real, I look at that and wonder if I'm missing something? The life that I've lived the past twenty years has given me an unrealistic idea of how love is supposed to be. So I wonder if I'll ever know. I guess I'll carry these insecurities with me forever. There's all different kinds of love in this world, the love you feel for your parents, children, family members, friends, and then hopefully there's that special someone. That's the one that consumes you within, burns out of control, forgiving, undying, everything in life brings you to that one feeling, the only thing that can fill that one particular void in your life, true love. There's no emptiness with love, only fulfillment in all the right places. We all want to share that with someone and hope that they share the same feeling. This is when you know you've got the real deal."

INFLUENTIAL PAIN

October 14, 2005
I awoke this morning, like many mornings, feeling empty…trying to hold on to my sanity if at all possible. I think about all the years that have come and gone and all the decisions I've made in the past, the people I have hurt without knowledge. It seems like the only company I've been able to keep is misery. It's not like it's something I'm not used to. I've always seemed to pick men that have led me down the path of misery. It's funny how you learn to pick that person out and cling on to that, thinking that it's different. This is what I'm used to, so it's hard for me to let go of the only thing I've ever known. About nine years ago I thought I had finally found the real deal. I got involved with someone I had known for a good while, he was nothing like I remembered in high school. The first nine months would be great. Blinded by passion, I foolishly let someone in. I wrapped myself up in this man; he had gotten me right where he wanted me. But I found out he was nothing like I remembered in high school. Now only misery begins. He was in control, a promise I made to myself that I would never let happen. Well, it happened. I desperately search for a way to get over the fear. You can't hold onto all the pain you've ever felt or you will explode."

October 29, 2005 MAN
"The immortal soul that connects to our hearts then becomes part of our soul. When this happens, the more I know the less I understand, I'm learning all over again. If I could turn the page in time, I would rearrange a day or two. No more broken hearts. It's like searching for a pot of gold, you know the kind you find at the end of the rainbow. Don't stop thinking about tomorrow, it'll be better than before, yesterday is already gone."

QUOTES

February 02, 2006
"I've looked back at my life now. I would've never guessed that a part of my life that lasted probably less than a minute, would change it forever. I was just starting to begin to know what life was all about, it was taken away from me in an instant. The journey that I now would begin, the physical, mental emotional toll and the scars that would not heal for years to come. I, at age thirteen, began experiencing horror I would go through. The thought has never left my mind, and I know it never will. But now looking back at the journey I've been led on, all the decisions I made, I wonder whether they were right or wrong. I now know where I want to go. At age thirty-eight, I finally know what's important, what I want and where my dreams will lead me. It's said that there's a destiny for you from GOD when you're born. For a long time I wondered why I suffered and made bad decisions, now I've accepted that so I can move on. The experience and having God in my life now, the knowledge he has given me, I'm not sure if I would change a thing. What I carry with me now will never change. He has carried me to this point in my life and he will decide my destination. The way things look now, my dreams are finally coming true."

March 8, 2006
"Writing this quote has been one of my most difficult. For two days I thought of what I wanted to say, but being able to put it down on paper is the hardest part. I'm going to give it a shot anyway. First of all I need to thank a man whose name is Mr. Junior Bettles. Over a year ago I started this train ride. While riding this train, there were many different directions that the tracks could lead me. It began on the right track, then ended up sliding off toward another direction. During this time I would sink on the inside, totally lost. I felt like everything I had accomplished was gone in an instant. Then I picked up the phone and called. Always leaving a message for Mr. Bettles to call, never to fail returning my call. A few minutes on the phone or if he thought best I would come in earlier than scheduled. No matter what, by the

INFLUENTIAL PAIN

time I hung up the phone, well, the train was back on track again. No, I'm not in love with this man but he is my rock. Thank you, Mr. Junior Bettles. The train ride isn't over yet but when that day comes, I'll always remember who laid the tracks for me. With God and Mr. Bettles on my side I could not think of a better combination. Many thanks, for now I actually know who I am and what I want to be and where I want to go. Thank you God up above and a man named Mr. Junior Bettles."

April 8, 2006
"Children, the creation of man and woman, the trials, pain, laughter, smiles, bad days, good days and the joy a small heart can bring to life. That old saying, "they step on your feet when they're little and step on your heart when they get older." How true this is. There are many gifts that come with being a parent, but there is also the sorrow to endure as well. It's not something you ask for, It just comes along with the package. Being able to handle all the ups and downs are not as simple as most would like them to be. We can only protect and give what knowledge we know based on our childhood. Sure there are things we do differently than our parents. There is always one thing that you hated that your parents would do, and you swear you wouldn't do that. Some will do the same thing, some will not. Parenting is the one thing that doesn't come with a handbook. The question is: even if it did, would we use it, agree with it or disagree with it? I've chosen to do things a little differently than my parents. The little things would have meant more to me than anything. A simple hug, a whisper in your ear, "Mommy loves you." That one little sentence we all like to hear, "a job well done or I'm very proud of you." These things we did not hear enough—the things that are natural for my children to hear. Communication, a key to any door that you're willing to open, good or bad. Learn to share all the feelings with your children so they know how to feel, share their feelings in response, and that line of communication will never fade. It's a lifetime job of dedication, but

the payoff when they get older is so rewarding. Your child is able to feel comfortable enough to share what feels good and what feels bad or what hurts. You'll feel the pain with them and also the glory that comes along with the character that we play known as the 'parent.' The one thing I want to also do is stay in touch with my children within, both in sorrow or happiness. These things will never leave once they are bestowed; trust me, I know from experience."

June 25, 2006
"The day passes as do most. I stop and think a minute. We all tend to judge people by their outer appearance or make an opinion without even knowing what's on the inside. It's the same as if you were going to buy a book. We always look at the ones with fancy covers because it catches our eye. Before we read the book we already assume that it is good by looking at the cover. Then once we start reading it's not so interesting as it appears to be. It's the same with people. We've all had our own pain and our own stories to tell, but no matter what, the pain isn't any different. So just remember before you judge the book by the outer cover, take a look inside. The same with people, before you judge the outward appearance, just remember there's a story to tell. In that story is something that you fail to see. So before you pass judgment, stop and think a moment and remember they are as human as you are and have their own pain. Just be sure to always read what's on the inside and you'll find out that the one with perhaps not such an attractive appearance, will have more on the inside than the fancy cover ever will. So never pass judgment without reading your own book first."

July 5, 2006
"As the curtains opens, he walks out on the stage. People watch with a look of amazement, no one could look any more like Elvis. Then he begins to sing. After the first song, people are thinking this is

unbelievable, the voice of a legend. As he continues to perform people are on the edge of their seats and most out of their seats. During this performance, you will enjoy the feeling of laughter, joy, some will cry because of the natural high he creates. This is a moment that people will cherish and carry with them throughout their lifetime. This man delivers such a gift to the people that it overwhelms them. When the show comes to an end the crowd is so excited. They've received such a wonderful feeling from this man, they all patiently wait in line after the show just to have the pleasure to meet him and talk for a brief moment. As he signs the last autograph and they walk away, I see something else that everyone else fails to see. Something I wish everyone could see. A unique individual, soft spoken, grateful, thankful, patient, and who gives himself unselfishly. A man with many special gifts. A man that most would consider a great man of wealth. So when everyone wonders who is behind the curtain, I'm one that's never in doubt; always look beyond the cover. This man is Tate Raven."

July 27, 2006
"Today after my therapy session, I always think about what is discussed and the suggestions that are made in order for me to handle what will come in the future. It's like a puzzle. Almost two years ago I began trying to put this puzzle together. The first nine months would be the hardest. I thought I would never get the outer edge put together. While putting this outer edge together, Junior, my therapist, would put pieces in place whenever needed, so he made it possible for me to connect a few more pieces together by the time we had our next session. Now the outer edge is completed. Pieces are beginning to fill the inside, creating a picture I only could have dreamed of. I will take my time adding these pieces together. I only look forward to seeing what the picture will look like when all the pieces are completed."

July 29, 2006
"There would be a man who entered my life like a fog or mist, and would disappear and fade just as quickly as that misty shadow. This man holds a special place in my heart and weighs on my mind a lot through the hours that pass. There was a void in my life that he was able to fulfill without my recognition until it faded away. The time that was spent together brought me great joy and filled a need I desired but did not realize. Then I had to realize where my obligations stood, the responsibilities I have, and what is number one to me: my children. My week is dedicated to work and my family. I've just now begun to learn to try to make myself sociable, to have a life beyond my family and work. It's to let go of that comfort zone or maybe I'm pushing myself too hard. The only thing I know is the man in the mist is where I want to spend my time when able. I guess I'm grasping on to something that slipped upon me without recognition. I hope that he will be patient and find a way to understand where my obligations are. Surely he would take a moment and think of what was shared, that felt so natural and came so unexpectedly. If I could only express myself by using my mouth and letting people know how I feel, then I wouldn't create my own pain. I will always be grateful and cherish the time that was shared, that came from the man in the mist."

August 26, 2006 The Man of Authenticity:
"He's been in the political eye for years. He's stable and built a reputation for himself, to know him is not uncommon to anyone. He doesn't discriminate or go without helping anyone. The history of this man started with my family years ago. He would only help my parents to see that my brother, who was ill, would have the medical help he needed. The more I've talked and met with him in the past six months, I've learned another side, a side most probably don't see. As I've changed my life, he's now helping me hopefully change the lives of others. He's sincere, dependable and gives without hesitation. Compassion is a rare gift. A man so indulgently has this rare

gift that makes him unique. I only look forward to see how the future will change as he continues to stay in office. Only good things are to come. He is pure and authentic. It's a pleasure to be his friend. SENATOR BOBBY GLOVER."

September 9, 2006
"As I sit and look out the window, I watch as people come and go through the neighbor's house. There has been a death. The death of a man who would only be thirty nine...I just so happen to be the same age. I have small children; he has small children. A man of few words, mentally unstable, but so strong-willed in mind to take his own life. Something for which his family will pay the price. Those who had parents do not understand how blessed they are. His children will only fight and seek for answers when there will not be any to give. No one's life is worth so little. Always think of those who love you. I hope that no children would suffer from a pain that scars for life. I know, I have one of those scars. In memory of J. Milton. 01-08-1967."

August 30, 2006
"As I drive away from a friend's house, I think about what friendship means and that old saying, "If you have three people through your lifetime you can call your friend, you're a wealthy person." I guess I'm fortunate: I have two, one female and one male. Friendship is a commitment, the same type of commitment as marriage. What is a friend? Someone who cares about you, loves you, someone you can depend on and someone you can rely on. They're not judgmental but support you and stand beside you through all the ups and downs. If people worked and treated their spouses as their friend first, it would be amazing how long marriages would last. I'm proud to say that Danny has been there fourteen years as a true friend. Mandy has been there going on twenty-one years. They're my family and always will

be. I'm thankful and blessed that they are a part of my life. I will carry them with me always as they have done for me. This is a gift most would take advantage of, a gift I plan to share with them throughout the rest of my lifetime."

www.ingramcontent.com/pod-product-compliance
Lightning Source LLC
Chambersburg PA
CBHW022110160426
43198CB00008B/419